Unholy Ghost

Unholy Ghost

Poems by

Nancy Jean Hill

Nancy Jean Hill

5/16/2017
For Jim + Elena,
Thank you so much
for having us to your home...

Kelsay Books

© 2016 Nancy Jean Hill. All rights reserved. This material may not be reproduced in any form, published, reprinted, recorded, performed, broadcast, rewritten or redistributed without the explicit permission of Nancy Jean Hill. All such actions are strictly prohibited by law.

Cover design: Bonnie Periale
Author photograph: Joseph Perna

ISBN 978-1-945752-05-6

Kelsay Books
Aldrich Press
www.kelsaybooks.com

For Baron, friend and mentor, who encouraged me
to keep on writing these poems

Acknowledgments

Grateful acknowledgment is made to the following publications in which some of these poems first appeared, sometimes in different versions.

Beryllium Diary, a chapbook, first published by Pudding House, 2007 and rereleased by Igneus Press, 2015: "Beryllium Diary," "Mother's Piano," "Whiskey Tears," "Some Things a Daughter Shouldn't Know," and "Teaching Mother to Swim."

The Café Review: "Dead-Dog Grief"

Edge: "There Was an Old Woman"

Currents V, Award winning poetry, fiction, and essays from the Seacoast Writers Association: "Heart Attack Number One"

Omphalos: "Mother-to-Be," "To the Dilator," "Cutting Off my Right Hand," and "Hummingbird"

Portsmouth Poet Laureate Postcard Project: "Fever"

Slipstream: "While Our Lungs are Collapsing"

I would also like to thank the directors and all the poets I met and worked with at The Frost Place in Franconia, New Hampshire, who for years validated me as a poet and gave feedback that helped me to improve my work.

Thanks also to all the members of the workshop, City Hall Poets, in Portsmouth, New Hampshire, for their invaluable critiques along the way.

And I would also like to acknowledge, with gratitude for Jane Kenyon's work, that the idea for the title poem of this book came to me after reading her poem "Having It Out with Melancholy," where she addresses melancholy as the "unholy ghost."

Contents

I.

The Man in Her Bedroom Closet	15
Another One of Your Games	16
Mother's Piano	17
Tonsillectomy, 1958	18
Unholy Ghost	20
The World According to My Husband	27

II.

In the Face of AIDS	31
Cutting Off My Right Hand	32
Some Things a Daughter Shouldn't Know	34
Dead-Dog Grief	35
How to Forgive Your Parents	37
Coming Together at Portsmouth Pavilion	39
Winter of the Long Goodbye	41
There Was an Old Woman	42

III.

Mrs. McNamara	45
While Our Lungs Are Collapsing	47
To the Dilator	49
After Three Decades	51
Photograph of My Friend, Steven	52
Beryllium Diary	53
Whiskey Tears	62

IV.

Teaching Mother to Swim	65
Heart Attack Number One	66
Hummingbird	67
Grandmother's House	69
Womb	71
Hula Dance	75
Mother-to-be	77
Fever	79

I.

The Man in Her Bedroom Closet

Some consider her a brave old woman,
but deep down she's a quaking child
who knows the man in her bedroom closet
will emerge in the eye of the night.

Deep down she's a quaking child
made to touch a dragon's fire
in the eye of the blackest night
when a man in a pinstriped suit

spewing a dragon's fire
slips between soft cotton sheets
handsome in his pinstriped suit
and gazes with crazed desire

at the girl between soft cotton sheets
who knows — though her eyes stay shut.
She rolls away from his crazed desire
and prays for morning to come.

She knows — though her eyes stay shut —
the fire he'll beg her to touch.
She prays for morning to come
when sunlight will scare him away.

She knows the fire he'll beg her to touch
and cringes when he takes her hand.
She waits for the sun to scare him away
and tries not to tremble or cry.

She cringes when he takes her hand.
This man from her bedroom closet
has the power to make her cry.
I consider her a brave old woman.

Another One of Your Games

The smirk on your face,
the husk in your voice,
the squeeze of your grip
still irk like the needle
on a scratched record.

My little-girl wrist held prisoner
by your big-man grasp
like an accused's neck in a stockade,
and I knew you wouldn't be satisfied
until I cried out for mercy:

LET ME GO!

Your voice mocked me
like a demented Pavoratti:

Let me go; let me go; let me go, Lover.

I hated the song and its implication,
but I knew the game wouldn't finish
until I played it your way, so I twisted
and squealed and wrenched and writhed,
and your hand became the jaw of a dog
playing tug, my wrist its rawhide toy.

I never knew when you'd let go,
but you always did, making me
the loser of this game, with my legs
flailing in the tepid air, Sunday dress
shrouding my face, concealing my tears,
butt planted firmly on the cold kitchen floor.

Mother's Piano

The Wurlitzer, once my mother's refuge,
grief's balm, an outlet for her rage
against God, stands silent in a corner of my den,
a child punished for speaking out of turn.
I can't bring it back in tune with years past
when Mother and I sat, hips touching, hands
brushing, and arpeggioed our way to happy.
Or to the days when she played and I sang:
Now is the Hour; *Ivory Tower*; *I Believe;*
and I wanted to believe
Mother would come down
from her own ivory tower,
touch her cool lips to my forehead
the way she did when my sister wasn't dead.

When my sister wasn't dead,
Mother got up in the morning.
Poured cereal and milk into depression-era
glass bowls, scrambled eggs on the gas stove.
She bundled us up in wool leggings, matching plaid coats
and sent us out to make *angel sisters* in the snow.
When our faces were chilled and mittens wet
she brought us hot chocolate topped
with marshmallow fluff; I can taste it still.
When my sister wasn't dead, Mother played
Silent Night — It Came Upon the Midnight Clear—
and year after year on Christmas Eve,
my sister and I would sing
Glory   to our mother's benevolent King.

Tonsillectomy, 1958

A woman wearing a mask smothers
you with a rubber dome, demands a deep
breath. Ether's sting carries you into grayness
where your father's face is a shadow.
Some part of you wants to speak
to him, but your voice box is a frozen pond.

You skate across the lonesome pond
wearing a pink woolen scarf, smothering
that part of you that wants to speak
out loud the secrets hidden in the depth
of your house and about the shadow
of booze beneath the roof's steel gray.

You float further into this land of gray
where drunk grandparents swim in a pond
naked, and you are watching in the shadows.
Slurred laughter and dirty words smother
whatever voice you ever had in the depth
of your throat, too sore to speak.

You wake up in the desert of no speech.
Your throat is on fire and your father's gray
eyes look as though they see your deep
desire to dredge the private pond.
The look on his bloated face smothers
you, seen and not heard, a shadow.

In a week's time, you are home in the shade
of a merciful weeping willow, speaking
in a whisper to your dolls, smothering
their porcelain faces in heavy gray

blankets so they can't smell the scary pond,
and then, your father's cigarette voice, deeper

than his sunken eyes, deeper
than your grandmother's grave, shadow
that makes you want to leap into a pond
so you never need to hear him speak
again, forever drowning the gray
rants, the blood-rage that smothers

the deep pond of your heart. He speaks to you
of his own shadows: smothering mother, staggering father —
and his gray eyes weep bourbon tears.

Unholy Ghost

when we were alone, you lay down
on top of me, pressing
the bile of desolation into every pore.

    —Jane Kenyon, from "Having It Out with Melancholy"

1. Sister

Your sister is dead and so should you be,
You, Unholy Ghost, said as you sat
on my bed's tucked edge
morning and night when I was three.
Nothing on this earth could save me.
Not the swaying of my bucket swing
while Mommy pushed me, nor the aroma
of Mimi's molasses cookies baking.
Not the guardian limbs of weeping willows
nor the prickly hedge that walled me off
from the barbed tongues of next-door bullies.

Your sister is dead and so should you be, You said.
Nothing on this unholy earth could save me.
By second grade, I was completely Yours,
though I won the spelling bee every week,
and Miss Levine, with the shimmery orange hair,
pasted silver stars on my pale, insensate cheek.

2. Father

Father loved to snap the strap of my bra
after supper while I washed and he dried,
loved to sting my rounding ass
with a quick snap of the dish towel.
Often I would raucously laugh and snatch

the stiffened towel from his grisly grip
but I was never any good at snapping,
my weapon an impotent wave in the anxious air.

It was the day I wore a tightly woven mini
he first called me a whore,
sat me down beside him on the couch,
knuckleballed my branded, bony knee.
This is what you need to watch for
is what he said as his dry hand
crept up my thigh to show me how
a lecherous boy might try to trick me.

And You, Unholy Ghost, proclaimed:
Just what you deserve, dressed like that.

3. College

You followed me to the small-town campus
where I fell in love with Odysseus,
accompanied him to the land of the dead
and tried to persuade my sister's shade to drink
from the pit my hero had diligently filled
with the spilled blood of a lamb, still bleating.
When my sister would neither swallow nor speak,
I abandoned my wandering lover, lay down
for a long while with Wordsworth,
held his head against my chest and grieved
with him his precious Lucy's death.

My sister's shade approached me then.

I felt her hand upon my heart.
She could not speak; I could not weep;
the weight was more than I could bear.
Your sister is dead and cannot save you
You said, and with a smile, enticed me
to plunge into a long-necked bottle.

4. Marriage and Babies

Hung over, yet able to stand
on the edge of Your quicksand pit,
I met a man staunch as dawn
who talked me out of jumping.

And the babies he gave me!
The fierce, miraculous pushing
that pulled me out of shameful sludge,
and lifted my sullied heart toward heaven!

But like a private eye with extra time,
You sniffed me out and found me
lolling in this clear, contented sea
and hauled me to a wailing cave
where women lay like dry fetuses.

They'd all be better off without you,
is what You said, and I wanted
to slap you dead, then shred
your impetuous tongue.

5. Sleep

When I couldn't get drunk
and couldn't stay sober, sleep
became my drug of choice.
I dreamt of endless hours of ten below,
of limber bottles dancing in the snow
with corpulent, crazy, squawking crows.
I dreamt of women sprouting raven wings
and giving birth to hawks.

But when I woke, it was You, Unholy Ghost,
who swilled at my engorged, marital breast.
You will never be free is what you said
after I shoved You out of my unwilling bed.
I bathed the children and washed their clothes.
I brewed the coffee and buttered the toast.
I hugged my husband and laughed at his jokes.

6. Rock-a-bye

My forty-year-old arms
rocked a bear named Huggins
with the might of a tortured child.

Take this cup and drink from it,
You said, and when I wouldn't drink,
You sent me back to Lothrop Street
where I watched a girl weeping
while sitting on the edge
of her father's rumpled bed.

I rocked, and I rocked

to-and-fro— to-and-fro—
'til the tenuous bough broke.

7. Conversation with My Husband

He says: Why don't you try an antidepressant?

(*NOTHING ON THIS EARTH WILL SAVE YOU.*)

I say: I should be able to pick myself up by the bootstraps.

He says: But you can't bend over.

I say: My wounds go deep

as Goliath's grave.

He says: But what about me and the kids?
Aren't we worth living for?

I say: The woman you married is already dead.

He says: No . . .

8. Inpatient

One nurse rummages through my bag
as though I were a terrorist
bent on blowing up psyche wards.

These razors will need to be locked up.
Another fires questions. Bleak bullets
turn me into a frozen heap
on a narrow, unmerciful mattress.

Suicidal thoughts?

        Yes.

Do you have a plan?

        Not since you locked up my razors.

When was your last drink?

        A long time ago.

Incest? Sexual Abuse?

        Maybe.

9. Ghost Slayer

There came a doctor's thunder,
Unholy Ghost, that silenced Yours
the way the ocean's pounding
drowns out a gull's squalling.

You can't go over, under, or around:
there's no way out but through.
Forgiveness is not condoning.
Forgiveness is the gift of letting go.

In spite of rising disbelief,
I donned a novice diver's tank
and dove into the whirling depths
of ancient, riptide sorrow.

I turned up Father's empty nips
and Mother's poisoned face.
I dug up my sister's grave
and scooped out healing grace.

10. Loons

When Your savage sucking finally stopped,
Unholy Ghost, I found myself gliding—
a buoyant bird with solid bones.
You're crazy as a love-struck loon,
is what You said as I floated by.
Your sister is dead and so should you be.

But I kept on paddling faithfully
and diving for my daily bread.
And when You tried again one night
to slip your noose around my neck
my sister Karen's shade appeared
above my quivering bed.
I heard her haunting call:
Love never dies, is what she said.
Love never dies.

The World According to My Husband

If a poem doesn't rhyme, it's not a poem.
If a radio station wanders into blues or jazz,
he turns the knob. If a novel meanders
away from plot, he closes the book.
For years I thought: no poet resides within him;
no tenor longs to sing God's praise.

But one evening, hands immersed in the suds
of supper dishes, I heard mockingbirds calling
to one another. Joy bounced back and forth
like voices of children playing hide-and-seek
on the first evening of daylight savings time
when bedtime is delayed for one glorious hour.
Hands dripping, I walked to the window,
saw my husband sitting on the porch —
whistling   and waiting—whistling   and waiting

II.

In the Face of AIDS

for Steven, 1951–1998

Shoulders sit like camels' humps
evenly spaced on either side
of your head which is proud
and erect, but sometimes teetering.
Your head has grown too big
for your neck, or is it your neck
has grown too small for your head?

You try to rise to the occasion,
to be a gracious host in your hospital-home,
but your fluid-filled-nerve-dead legs
betray you the way the heroin did
when you were sixteen.

Olive-brown skin deceives me
into thinking you've been lying
in the sun, but there is no sun
where you are, is there?
Only guinea-pig cocktails
coursing through your rebellious veins,
poisoning while claiming to heal.

Your features stare me down.
Your nose bigger than I recall.
Ears an intrusion, eyes
a deeper, anguished blue.
So deep, I feel myself sinking
into them, seeing me
for what I have become
to you.

Just another pinprick
in your uncushioned, sunless world.

Cutting Off My Right Hand

*and if your right hand is a cause of trouble to you,
let it be cut off and put it away from you;
because it is better to undergo the loss of one part,
than for all your body to go into hell.*
   —Matthew 5:30

A week ago, I dropped a crystal platter.
Cried when it cracked against ceramic.
I wanted to use the shards, then and there,
to cut off my clumsy right hand
but went upstairs and brushed my daughter's hair
one hundred frenzied strokes instead.

One hundred frenzied strokes.
Yesterday, I was folding clothes,
slipped my hand into the pissing
slit in my husband's cotton boxers.
Fell back into my father's waiting lap
and the gap in his gray pajamas.

He held my hand, would not let go,
then cleared his raspy throat:
*That good-for-nothing college boy
so much as touches your tits
and I'll bust open his fucking head
with my steel-shafted pitching wedge.*

That good-for-nothing college boy
once drove me to the peak of lover's lane.
Asked me to unzip his faded jeans.
Begged me to hold his penis in my hand.
Taught me how to pump out pain
in the back seat of a '66 Mustang.

Fervent engine still hot
we pulled into my yard
and Father, face flushed, gray pajamas gaping,
slammed the storm door, rushed out,
captured my reluctant right hand,
pressed it to his spider-veined cheek.

That good-for-nothing college boy smiled.
Stared past the steering wheel
into his own cutting desires
where sons killed fathers
who slapped mothers
and it was a man's right to drink.

It comes at odd times, this ability to smile.
You can see it in good-for-nothing college boys
wearing far too many shades of blue.
You can see it in old photos: sepia or black and white.
Fathers holding daughters too tight.
Daughters obediently smiling.

Some Things a Daughter Shouldn't Know

My father,
a pharmacist's mate
in the United States Navy,
called himself a pecker-checker.

Sailors lined up
penises exposed
to the sea breeze
while Father checked
for discharge and sores,
administered shots.
A World War II hero
saving lives daily.

He brought crabs home
to his callow wife.

Dead-Dog Grief

Consider, if you will, a middle-aged man
scattering ashes into a wicked winter sea
while his wife stays in their marital grave
wearing a feather pillow over her head,
snuffing out visions of loyal dogs, now dead,
shutting up the perpetual bark of grief.

Consider the hunching down of grief
and all the tears wept by a man
who carries to the shore's edge dead-
dog ashes and scatters them into the sea
while scavengers swoop from overhead
hoping to be nourished by the grave

nature of this man's grave
errand. Consider what grief
he feels. Never getting ahead.
Never being the kind of man
who could rise above the sea
and save his dogs from being dead.

All of his passion spent on three dead
dogs and his marriage digging its own grave
the way his dogs dug for bird bones by the sea
and came up with nothing but grief,
the merciless snap of sand crabs, making the man
want to cut off the little creatures' heads.

Tearing of the flesh and mutual beheading—
words that dripped with irreconcilable grief—
the onerous path of this wife and her sad man.
Dogs that saved the marriage gone to their graves.

Ashes kept in urns for years. Dead
love—dead dogs—thrown into the sea.

Ashes vanish like ghosts into the churning sea.
Beach walkers, shell seekers, turn their heads
toward the water's edge and grieve
the many years they've spent in deadly
quarantine, never realizing the grave
needs of lonely men.

The silence of a dying sea echoes like grief.
A man wades toward a salty grave.
Awakened witnesses bow their heads.

How to Forgive Your Parents

I.

Creep into the shady corners of your childhood home.
Eat at the table where slurred speech spoiled your appetite.
Lie on the couch where your father's hand roamed
from your knee to your upper thigh. Scrutinize
sepia photos. Notice how he held you tightly
and she let him, how your smile is forced.
Skip down Lothrop Street. Listen for his wolf-whistle.
Spin around. Flip him the bird.

If forgiveness still eludes you (as it probably will),
buy a punching bag and hang it in the cellar.
Jab away. Pretend it's him. Pretend it's her,
your mother, who stayed in bed day after day.
Venture outside and kick some rocks
all the way to the bottom of the drive.
Dig a garden. Plant grief. Pull up anger.

II.

Plant grief, pull up anger, and when the rage
feels fully spent, step into the forgotten light
of your childhood home and tread barefoot
on crew-cut grass where your father taught you
to putt and chip. Swing from the thick rope
he hung from the giant oak. Cycle down
Sheridan Street where he held you steady
on your two-wheel bike then lovingly set you free.

If all of this is not enough, kneel on the kitchen floor
where you and your mother played pick-up-sticks.
Brush your hand across the wing-backed chair
where she showed you how to purl and knit.
Caress the wooden spoon she stirred with.
Then finger the Wurlitzer's lonely keys.

III.

Finger the Wurlitzer's lonely keys
and sing the songs learned on your father's knee.
Knit little mittens like your mother did
and think less of the things she used to forbid.
Remember instead the nights she brushed
sweaty bangs from your fevered forehead,
rubbed out cramps from your fast-growing legs,
cut out paper dolls on the edge of your bed.

And when your own baby's vomit spews across the kitchen
and her croupy cough launches you into a mother's fret
remember the nights he cradled you in a steamy bath,
put down his glass of bourbon so you could breathe.
And remember how often he tried to quit.
Then shut the door and listen for its firm click.

Coming Together at Portsmouth Pavilion

Major Depression—
                    Manic Depression—
Schizophrenia—
                Agoraphobia—
Neurosis—
        Psychosis—

Xanax—
        Prozac—

Depacote—
        Lithium—
Zoloft—
        Klonapin—

My roommate,
          an unknown number

of persons
        jigsawed,   an artist
starved
            for a cure

etches endorphin
            maps
of her world
        into
              stick-figure
forearms

    hands trembling
                         like a drunk
without
        a drink
                she concocts
her own remedy

finger-painting   after finger-painting
            red and runny
                        as head-injury blood
on construction paper
                        black
as fresh tar

Wallpaper
              for our gray-filled room
where we swallow
                    pills
with sips of water
                from a tiny paper cup.

Winter of the Long Goodbye

This long goodbye is like the melting snow—
In spring it causes floods that drown the river rats.
This long goodbye resembles undertow—
The swirling hopelessness cannot be matched.
It's brought me down and spit me out like bait.
It's wiped me clean of all defiant pride.
It's helped me comprehend the urge to hate.
It's made me curse the day I stood, a bride.

If a prophet had foretold these winter throes
I would have cut his scathing tongue in two—
And let it bleed until it clogged his throat.
This long goodbye is a puss-filled wound—
Green and thick—slowly seeping—
So much pain, so much weeping.

There Was an Old Woman

who chatted with the ants
that nested in her lazy-susan each June
and cheerfully wiped up paw prints
from her kitchen floor and laughed
at the mouse who peeked out
from her pot-holder drawer
and her elbows were as crusty
as a crotchety old man
and she couldn't care less
about meticulously made beds
and she threw open her blinds
allowing bright brocade to fade
and she drove in the snow
with wide open eyes.

III.

Mrs. McNamara

On Tuesdays, when I was five,
not long after my sister died,
I removed my dirty shoes
and crackled across carpet
covered by the daily news

to the dreaded wooden bench
where Mrs. McNamara,
a human metronome,
counted out quarter-time
in a threatening tone

then molded my stiff fingers
into kittens' claws, curved
and ready to pounce and play
made-easy Beethoven and Brahms
but never the way my sister played.

My sister, Mrs. McNamara's lump
of musical clay, had practiced
the mandatory hour every day.
She never seemed to mind at all
being Mrs. Mac's prodigy doll.

All dolled up in inherited frills,
I played scales against my will
on Tuesdays, when I was five,
worked hard for my weekly prize:
one white mint that always stung
then a pink and soothing one.

On Tuesdays, when I was five,
not long after my sister died,
Click after Click after Click
Mrs. McNamara doled out time
with a twelve-inch stick.

While Our Lungs Are Collapsing

I left my toddlers each week to visit you.
Seeing you, so small and almost blue
in your king-sized bed, eyes wide
with the struggle to breathe,
always brought me to my knees.

On the day you almost died,
I was doing your hair
when you began to rant
about Dad's refusal to make love
to you, to *slip it in the back way*.

I wanted to slap my hand
over your mouth, to end it all.

And then your left lung collapsed.
I carried you, light and limp,
but still ranting about Dad,
placed you in my Subaru and drove,
cursing at drivers obeying the speed limit.

You grabbed air with one lung
and with both hands yanked
brush rollers from your hair.
I can't let anyone see me like this
you said, and begged me for a comb.

Curlers rolled around the dashboard,
tumbled to the floor, when I veered
onto Hospital Road, where they
punctured your chest—
inflated your lung—

while I knelt and prayed
for this to be the last time,
my own lungs expanding
as though they were in your chest.

To the Dilator

I know you followed doctor's orders.
I was there. Face down on the stainless steel
table—exposed. I heard the doctor say:
*Daily dilation will cure your daughter's
constipation,* and I heard the rest
of the diagnosis: *fissures—*
though I thought he said fishes,
so my little-girl mind embarked
     on a journey
       into my own bowels—
envisioned finned creatures
        swimming
        inside me
 peeing and pooping
slurping and swallowing
   my reluctant blood.

I know you followed doctor's orders.
 I was there when he probed
 and I heard the diagnosis.
     But Father,
  the stink of bourbon
  on any man's breath
    still hurls me
  onto a twin bed
  in the back room
of a cedar-shingled cottage
    on Cape Cod

  where for two weeks straight
  when I was nine, you interrupted
highballs every day at five o'clock

sharp, the door ajar so company
could hear, you stretched
my anus with something rubber
slimed with Vaseline
then bellowed
in slurred speech:

Greetings Gates, let's dilate.

I flailed at the friction
in your raspy voice,
flipped
my pearly backside
the way an almost-dead fish
still flips its tail
and then

I sank
into the soft center
of my bed,
broke through the surface
that separates
black waters from light
and swam, Father,
a silver-bellied mackerel
set free
into a distant rainbow world.

After Three Decades

He adores the constancy of his wife,
how she sips green tea reverently
each evening, basking in the heat of it.
He dreads the day she'll go away.

She sips green tea reverently
counting grandbaby-bunting stitches.
He knows one day she'll go away
though today she sits in the room knitting.

She counts grandbaby-bunting stitches.
He glares at round-ball players running.
She lays down her knitting.
Pulse drumming for a luscious lover.

He glares at round-ball players running.
She offers bravely a bared breast.
Her pulse drums for a luscious lover.
Her nipples crave a titillating tongue.

She offers bravely a bared breast.
His favored team engaged in sudden death.
Her nipples crave a titillating tongue.
At stake—his point-spread wager.

His favored team engaged in sudden death
on this bleak-as-losing-streak evening.
At stake—his point-spread wager.
Ten-to-one the odds against his wanting.

On this bleak-as-losing-streak evening
she is basking in the heat of need.
Ten-to-one the odds against his wanting.
He adores his wife, her constancy.

Photograph of My Friend, Steven

He is lying on his side
in the middle of my hallway
and what makes it laughable
is the cordless phone to his ear
and the fact he wields a yardstick

as he attempts to coax a mouse
from under the baseboard heat
while at the same time
animatedly conversing
with his mother, Louise,

telling her about our golf match,
bragging about his grooved swing,
still wearing the sapphire-blue cap
that accentuates his *om namah shivaya*
eyes, and his shorts have ridden up
to expose the end of his golfer's tan.

Last night, I watched him dance
with his Cassandra to *Unchained Melody*.
She, a married woman and he, a victim
of AIDS, both knowing this would be
the closest they would ever come
to satisfying their mutual hunger.

In a year's time, his hard muscles will shrivel,
bones seeming to take their place.
Supple lips will crack like dried-up mud,
and his tongue will throb with thrush
the way his mother's heart drums now
that he no longer sits in her living room,
draped in a crocheted prayer shawl, chanting.

Beryllium Diary

for my mother, 1924–1980

1.

1943.
Men in coveralls
in Salem, Massachusetts
prolong the life
of fluorescent lighting tubes,
coat them with miraculous metal—
atomic weight of only nine—
while secretaries on their way
to lunch stroll past the coating room.

Mother is nineteen years old,
strolling with the others,
oblivious to the dust
seeping into her lungs
like midges through a screen
on a thick, humid night.

Men bring home coveralls
for their wives to wash.
Wives grow tired, breathless.
Develop coughs
dry as August drought.

Twenty-two thousand people
move to a secret city
in rural Tennessee.
Worker bees in a government hive.
Manhattan Project the buzz.

Y-12 Weapons Plant opens its doors
to men in coveralls, paid well,
oblivious to the facts:
they are being used
to build Little Boy.

1945.
Mother marries a pharmacist's mate
in the United States Navy, oblivious
to the cobwebs spreading
inside her lungs.
Little Boy ends the War
the way Armageddon
will end the world.

1947.
The Cold War begins.
A weapons plant in rural Tennessee
uses beryllium—
lighter than aluminum—
stiffer than steel—
to build better atomic bombs.
Elemental miracle shipped
from a plant in Lorain, Ohio
where neighbors complain
of unexplained
shortness of breath.

Meanwhile, men in coveralls
in Salem, Massachusetts drop
like sprayed hornets:
Acute Beryllium Disease.

Wives who sorted and washed
their clothes grow warty bumps,
wake before dawn drenched
in sweat like worn-out soldiers
home from the trenches.

Mother gives birth
to Karen Mae, oblivious
to the widespread scarring—
lung tissue thickening like honey.

2.

1948.
Headline:
*BERYLLIUM PLANT IN LORAIN, OHIO
DESTROYED BY FIRE*: Atomic Energy
Commission makes deal with executive:
*We will rebuild if you will provide
all the beryllium we need.*

1950.
Mother is twenty-six years old.
Needs to rest every third
or fourth step
on her way to bed.
Develops a dry cough.
August drought.

Diagnosis: Chronic Berylliosis.
Pregnancy will worsen symptoms.

Could cause death to the mother.
Karen Mae will need to be an only child.

Treatment: Cortisone,
guinea-pig drug,
disturbs monthly cycle
and reshapes Mother
into a moon-faced stranger
who cannot climb a flight of stairs
without halting to catch her breath.
One of the lucky ones, doctors say.

1951.
New Year's Eve.
Mother has a few highballs.
Tells Father she feels something
fluttering in her belly.
Doctors confirm:
She is eighteen weeks pregnant.

Beryllium producers, termites gnawing
inside beams, work toward National Security.
Atomic Energy Commissioner states:
Unless instructed otherwise,
production comes first, then health.

May the 21st.
Baby Girl Thissell is born.
Four pounds, eleven ounces.
A week later named Nancy Jean.
Father lays warm compresses
on the place where Mother is torn.

1954.
The Cold War continues.
First batch of thermonuclear parts
assembled and shipped from Y-12.

Christmas Eve.
Mother's first daughter, Karen Mae,
fights for breath like a rabbit
struggling to free itself from a snare.
Emergency tracheotomy fails.
Karen Mae turns blue, dies.
No one can explain why.
Nancy Jean becomes the only child.

1968.
A nuclear machinist is hired into Y-12.
Told he will help to make
our country and our world a safer place.

Let's call him Mr. J: twenty years old
when beryllium dust invades
his workspace like riled up invisible bees.
Officials tell him beryllium is safe:
You can eat the stuff and it won't hurt you.

Mother and I go to Portsmouth
to shop for my Junior Prom gown.
Walking around the city strangles her.
She is losing her breath inch by inch
the way a burn victim sheds skin.

3.

1978.
The Occupational Safety and Health Administration
proposes a standard that will
reduce workers' exposure to beryllium dust.
Company executives in Cleveland, Ohio shoot
the standard down like a front-line enemy.
More workers begin the slow, painful death
by suffocation.

My three-year-old daughter, Amanda Jean,
lies on a hospital bed
and strokes her grandmother's blue hand.
My five-year-old son, Daniel Shane,
builds towers with Lincoln Logs
on the gray linoleum floor.
Mother is fifty-four.
Seventy-five pounds.
Her left lung collapsed
like a tire deflated
by shards of glass
that waited for decades
at the bend of a sharp curve.

1980.
Mr. J still doing quality inspection
of nuclear weapons components for Y-12.
Presents breathing problems.
Diagnosis: Asthma.

June the 18th.
Goodwin's Nursing Home.
Mother by far the youngest patient.
Father paces in the hallway
like a feral dog
confined to a cage.
I sit beside Mother's bed,
frantic fingers knitting.

Mother is having a good day.
Doctors have prescribed mood elevators.
Why didn't they give me these sooner?
She halts between each word,
sputters her way up
the impossibly steep hill.
Her next to last breath
a long sigh.

1993.
Mr. J is forty-five years old.
Still working for Y-12.
Breathing capacity dropping
the way mercury drops
after a cold front passes through.
Finally receives accurate diagnosis:
Chronic Beryllium Disease.
Berylliosis.
Beryllium Poisoning.

2004.
Mother would be eighty years old.
Her great-granddaughter, Aubrey Sage, is born.
Mr. J is fifty-six. Spends more time

in the hospital than out.
His breath shallow and moth-light.
His chest a raging furnace.

December.
Dog-day cicada song long gone.
Winter solstice close.
I am watching Headline News.
Mercury dropping.
*The President's Choice for America's Top Energy Post
spent fourteen years at the helm of a company
accused of decades-old beryllium poisoning.*

My fingers draw themselves
into a tight fist. Mother
would be eighty years old.
(that dry cough, her frail breath)
Mr. J still spends more time
in the hospital than out.
(chest a raging furnace)
Karen Mae—dead—
for half a century.

Energy officials express surprise
at the President's choice
for America's top energy post.
I throw open a window,
breathe in lung-freezing air.
Dog-day cicada song long gone.
Silence chills.
Are the stars safe?
Five decades of sorrow,

ache like an amputee's
phantom legs walked on
too far and far too long.

Whiskey Tears

The night the call came
that my mother had died, I sat
for two hours straight, still
as a tree stump, on top
of a cracked toilet tank
in a dank motel room,
feet planted like ancient roots
on the closed seat.

During the third hour,
I began rocking.
Then, the monotonous motion
of one lone limb lifting
whiskey and coke to quivering lips.
Terrible tasting stuff.
Good only for uncorking stoppers
behind unblinking eyes.

IV.

Teaching Mother to Swim

I was the one she trusted most
on that rare, blue-sky day
above the water, beside the boat.

I was the one who taught her to float
in the brine of Buzzard's Bay.
I was the one she trusted most.

She meandered through sea oats,
waded way past her waist,
head above water, beside the boat.

I demonstrated the side stroke,
showed her how to play.
I was the one she trusted most.

And even when she began to choke,
it was I who helped her stay
above the water, beside the boat.

The words *I love you* caught in her throat,
a phrase she could never say,
but I was the one she trusted most,
above the water, beside the boat.

Heart Attack Number One

Moments after your batch of home brew
burst in the basement, I found you rolling
on the floor, arms crossed, knees tucked,
the way you'd taught me to do if ever
I caught fire. I yelled for Mother,
who stumbled down cellar stairs,
housecoat agape, graying hair
askew — *Call an ambulance*, she said.

We visited you Easter morning
after church. Eager to please, I twirled
around your hospital room — purple
pleated skirt swirling around panty-hosed
legs, lily-white blouse boasting my first bra.
I was hoping to resurrect your smile.

You rose up from your bed, promised
to quit, and we (Mother and I)
envisioned salvation. Until the spring
of the following year, when you
built the bar in the basement,
knotty-pine all over, well stocked,
cracked crucifix on the back wall.

Hummingbird

for Steven, 1951–1998

A hummingbird darts toward pink
then away—again and again—
and flickering thoughts of you
flutter in and out like joy

and away—again and again.
Blue smoke swirls close
flutters in and out like joy.
Memorial Day gone by, and I forgot

the swirling cigarette smoke
from when I saw you last.
Memorial Day gone by, and I forgot
to plant pansies at your grave, yellow

like your skin when I saw you last,
your eyes still blue as Carolina sky,
and I placed pansies in your palms, yellow
and blue like the bruises on your arms.

We worshiped together the Carolina sky,
stood on a deck overlooking the sea,
green and gray, like an old bruise, and your arms
thin as twigs, pinched of all sap.

We stood on a deck overlooking the sea,
and you spoke of journeys you would never take.
Your were thin, pinched of all sap,
but still much stronger than me.

You spoke of journeys to the other side
while I had flickering thoughts:
You were always stronger than me,
a hummingbird darting toward pink.

Grandmother's House

A small girl sits in the back seat of a long, blue car
as her father drives though a live-oak tunnel
on the way to her grandmother's yellow house.
The girl hopes the cobwebby moss that hangs
from the trees has the power to shroud
her from the eyes of her wrinkled grandmother.

Two years since she hugged her grandmother
and that's all she can think about riding in the car.
How might she wrap herself up in a shroud?
Could she escape Grandmother's hugs by tunneling
her way through the sheets that usually hang
on the line beside the yellow house?

Someone opens a window in the house.
The hand that waves is her grandmother's.
The girl stares from afar at the flesh that hangs
and asks her mother, *Please, may I stay in the car?*
NO comes out of a long, black tunnel
and the girl's stuffed bear becomes her shroud.

Grandmother comes to the car carrying a shroud
of sheets she has pulled from the line beside the house.
The girl trudges through the live-oak tunnel
that leads to the door of her grandmother's
hugs and her grandfather hanging
his head in shame behind the wheel of a car.

Grandfather killed the boy next door with his red car
and Grandmother tried her best to shroud
him from the parents, who wanted a hanging.
Neighbors protested in front of the house

when they released him from jail, but Grandmother
held his hand and walked him through the human tunnel.

How long did Grandfather wander in this hateful tunnel?
Did he ever again sit behind the wheel of a car?
Questions the curious girl asked her grandmother
who told her some things must stay beneath the shroud
that has covered this sad, yellow house
since the day the girl found her grandfather hanging.

Hanging from the largest live oak in front of the house.
Grandmother sewing shrouds to bury the red car.
Live-oak roots digging tunnels beneath the scorched lawn.

Womb

I.

I have a tenacious itch and a killing pain.
Post-menopausal blood stains like kelp.
My gynecologist wants to snip
a piece of seaworthy endometrium,
but my weary cervix is stubborn.
Stuck shut like a storm-swollen door,
it says *I am done*.
But my doctor is determined.

She pries while I'm anesthetized.
Dilation and Curettage fails.
To collect the tissue she will need,
to know if cancer grows like a school of fish
where my two prized fetuses once grew,
she will need to remove my suspect womb.

II.

She will need to remove my suspect womb.
She will banish Daniel's haven,
the cove in which he found his sacred thumb.
She will steal the watery cave that stretched
its limits like a full-moon winter tide
awaiting the birth of brave Amanda Jean,
Goddess of stray cats and worm-filled dogs,
victim of infertility.

I have signed my authority over
to a smooth-skinned doctor, a mother

of five, four girls and a boy.
I have given her permission to take
a sterile knife and make a four-inch slice,
vertical, no bikini cut for me.

III.

A vertical slice, no bikini cut.
Might as well scoop out the ovaries, too.
Rotten, good-for-nothing eggs inside.
Little more than cancer-compost piles.
The bit of estrogen they leak
no better than a sprinkle in a drought.
No better than a trickle from a stream.
No better than a wad of spit for washing.

But what about the drench of nightly sweat,
the shrinking spine, the dreaded hump?
Taking estrogen by mouth will help.
But then, what about my breasts?
The chance I take of losing them as well?
This cold-hearted document gives consent . . .

IV.

This cold-hearted document gives consent
to take away my flat, unblemished belly.
Replace it with scarred and spongy flab.
I will say goodbye to moist and steamy loins.
Making love will hurt like squeaking chalk.
My phantom uterus will not contract.
My pleasure will be shorter and not so deep.

Sex will be supplanted by selfless work.
My emptied-woman state assuaged
by offering respite to old and weary wives
who live with terminally ill and grouchy husbands.
My moods will turn as black as widow's grief.
My husband will want to move away from me,
and I will go on wanting him   to stay.

V.

And I will go on wanting him to stay
the way I wanted him to stay that night
on the just-for-husbands pullout couch
in my chilly post-op hospital room.
But he was done with me,
my asking him to stay, absurd.
I need some food, a good night's sleep.

Just then, I heard the next-door newborns wail,
calling out for precious milk.
For one drugged moment, my empty breasts
let down and I cried out: *Bring me my baby!*
My husband shook his head in disbelief.
I waved my hand, allowing him to go.
He kissed my forehead, patted matted hair.

VI.

He kissed my forehead, patted matted hair
as though I were a pet, not wife of thirty years

and placed the nurses' buzzer in my hand
and I remembered Mother's face when I
walked out on her because I needed booze
and she with holes in her chest and tubes to breathe
showed worry in her eyes for me, and I
left anyway because I could not stay

the way she'd stayed with me when I
was six and could not breathe without a tent.
She stayed beside my bed for days and nights
until my shallow breath returned and then
she stayed some more until I laughed
out loud as though my breath had always been.

VII.

As though my breath had always been, I laughed
and wept when I heard the lab results.
A polyp, not cancer, had caused the blood.
And I knew right away that Karma wins,
that Karma always wins no matter what
we say or pray or try to do, it wins
though a woman in pain
wants her husband to stay.

When morphine seeps in like mania, and hives
break out like convicts, and the buzzer goes unanswered
and her skin is crawling with fire-ant armies
and her belly burns from inside out and the babies
keep on crying—a woman wants relief
from the tenacious itch and the killing pain.

Hula Dance

A girl twirls her way through curlicues of smoke.

She is seven years old—stripped.

Ice cubes clink against glass.

Stench of stale ash pervades.

Adults in a stupor hum.

Grandmama hands the girl

a purple, plastic hoop.

Urges her to sway scant hips.

Grandpapa wolf-whistles.

The girl spins faster.

Purple plastic bites bare skin.

The hoop falls.

Papa applauds.

The girl bows.

Grandpapa cups her chin in calloused hands.

Voulez-vous coucher avec moi ce soir?

The girl drops to her knees.

Time for bed, Mama rules.

Papa plucks her up.

Cradles her.

Carries her to a four-poster bed.

Tucks her in tightly.
Don't let the bed bugs bite.

The girl goes on dancing,

even in her dreams.

Goes on spinning and spinning

the hideous, hollow hoop.

Mother-to-be

for Mandy

In a gallery in Del Ray, I find a sculpture small enough
to carry home, but I decide
it is too dear. It is of a woman.
A black woman done in black-fired clay.

    At eight months pregnant I looked fourteen,
    though I was twenty-one.
    Every day I walked two miles to the market
    with a sack for carrying groceries.

The woman done in black-fired clay is nude and with child.
She is lying on her left side in that position
a pregnant woman takes when her belly has grown
too big to lie any other way.

    I don't know why—but sometimes I still lie
    in that position, though I am way past
    child bearing and my belly is fairly flat.

The black-fired clay woman's head is cradled in the crook
of her bent left arm and her right leg is bent
at nearly, but not quite, ninety degrees.

    At eight months pregnant I wore my husband's t-shirts
    and size thirty-four pants. Maternity clothes too dear
    except for the hand-me-down gold empire-waist dress I wore
    on Easter while playing croquet on my in-laws' pristine lawn.

The mother-to-be in black-fired clay is sleeping.
Her left leg is nearly, but not quite, straight—
leaving room for her big belly to breathe.

The Lamaze instructor taught my husband and me
how to breathe the breath of labor and I practiced
each day after walking home from the market.

The woman in black-fired clay has no furrow in her brow.
I look closer and see that she looks young—very young.
One could judge that she is too young to be pregnant.

> When I was pregnant with my first child, my brow
> often furrowed. Some people on the street
> looked away from me as if I were too much
> for their tender eyes to bear.

This woman in black-fired clay could be a teenager.
Or she could be twenty-one. Or she could be
like my young-looking, big-bellied daughter
who carried a barren weight into her thirties.

> When I walked into town carrying
> my big belly, some people stared.
> Others gave me dirty looks. Perhaps
> they thought I was a pregnant teen
> and should be living in a home for unwed mothers.

This woman in black-fired clay might be a teen—or she might be
twenty-one— or she might be like my daughter—
who has finally found
a comfortable position for sleeping.

Fever

for Bill

Could you come over and hold me
'til these teeth-chattering chills subside?
I will ask nothing more of you.
Just swaddle me in your arms
'til these fiery chills expire.

I'm breaking.
Top to bottom, piece by piece,
stained glass sung
to shattering by a chorus
of first sopranos.

Have you written that poem yet?
The one about cicadas invading
canals during December's snow?
Could you come over and read
to me until the drumming
in my ears disappears?

Am I half-crazed from gazing
at constellations through the skylight
above my bed?
I'm alone with my dog
and she's delirious, too.

Please—
could you come on over—
hold me—
'til these teeth-chattering chills subside?

About the Author

Nancy Jean Hill is the author of one previous book, *Beryllium Diary*, a chapbook first published by Pudding House in 2007 and rereleased by Igneus Press in 2015. She received both her Bachelor's in English and Master's in Education from Plymouth State College, where she later worked as a one-on-one writing consultant to students, faculty and staff. She lives and writes in Stratham, New Hampshire and Readfield, Maine.

p 70 - "Live oake roots digging tunnels beneath
          The scorched lawns."
pp 20-26 "Unholy Ghost" — The best one
p 27 - "The World According to My Husband"
  32 - "Cutting Off My Right Hand"
  37 - "How To Forgive your Parents"